SureShot Books
PUBLISHING LLC

Books have the power to change lives.

SureShot Books Publishing LLC is part of the SureShot 2k family of companies that was founded in 1990 to help inmates & their families by making it possible to improve their lives with the Power of Reading.

Here at SureShot Books, we fervently believe that the fact that you have made a mistake does and should not mean that your life is ruined forever.

We believe that everyone deserves a second chance.

Contact Us with any questions or concerns:
SureShot Books Publishing LLC
P.O. Box 924, Nyack, New York 10960
845.675.7505
Email Us:
info@sureshotbooks.com

This Notebook Belongs To

_____

_____

_____

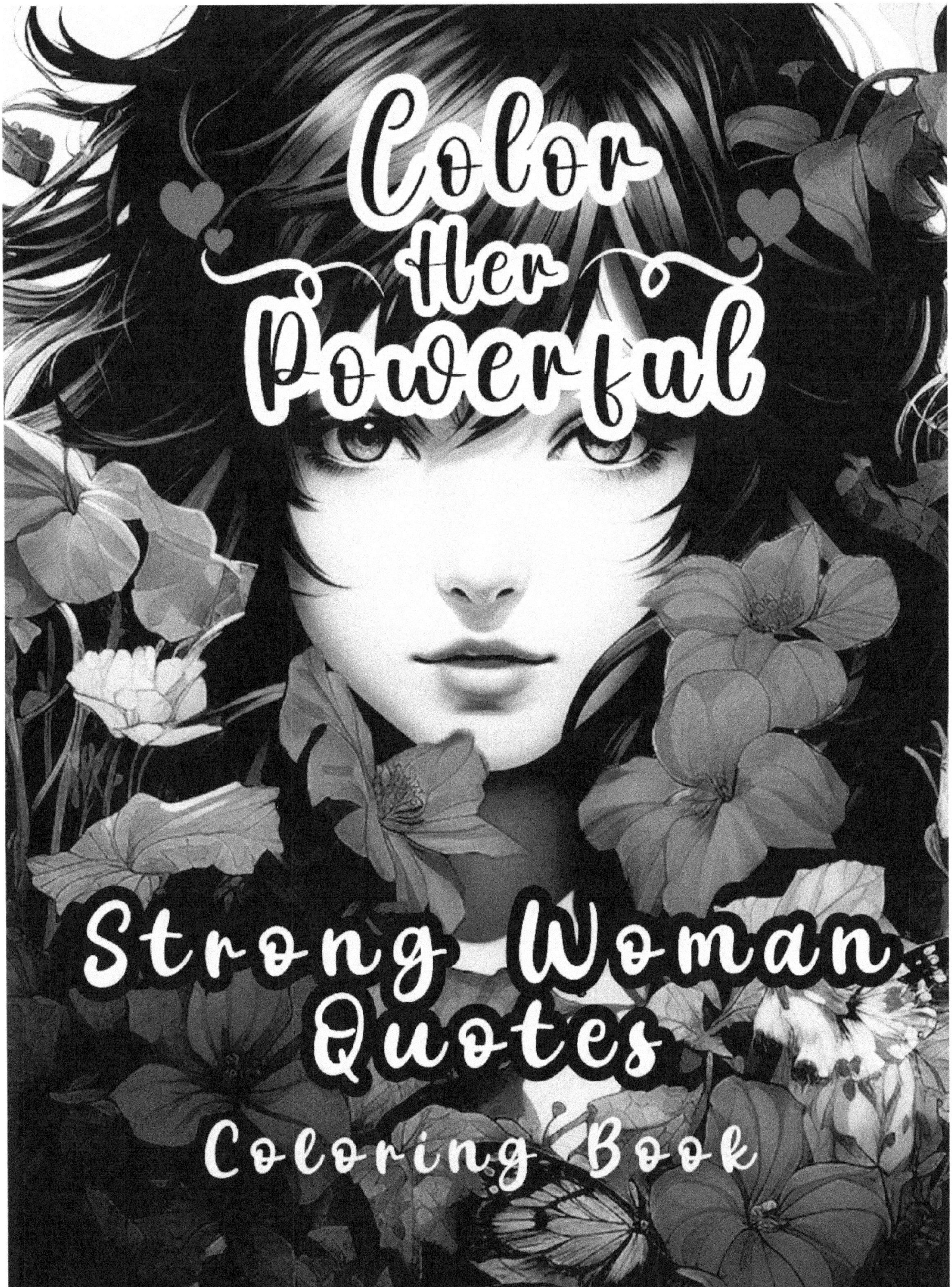
Color
Her
Powerful
Strong Woman
Quotes
Coloring Book

STRONG WOMAN

QUOTES COLORING BOOK

Empower your spirit with our 'Strong Woman Quotes Coloring Book.' Immerse yourself in a collection of inspiring quotes celebrating resilience, courage, and the indomitable strength of women. Each page is a canvas for your creativity, featuring powerful words paired with elegant illustrations. Whether you're a strong woman yourself, or you want to celebrate the fierce women in your life, this book is a tribute to the unyielding spirit of femininity. Uncover motivation, encouragement, and a sense of empowerment with every stroke of color. Embrace the beauty of strength and resilience as you bring these quotes to life in vibrant hues.

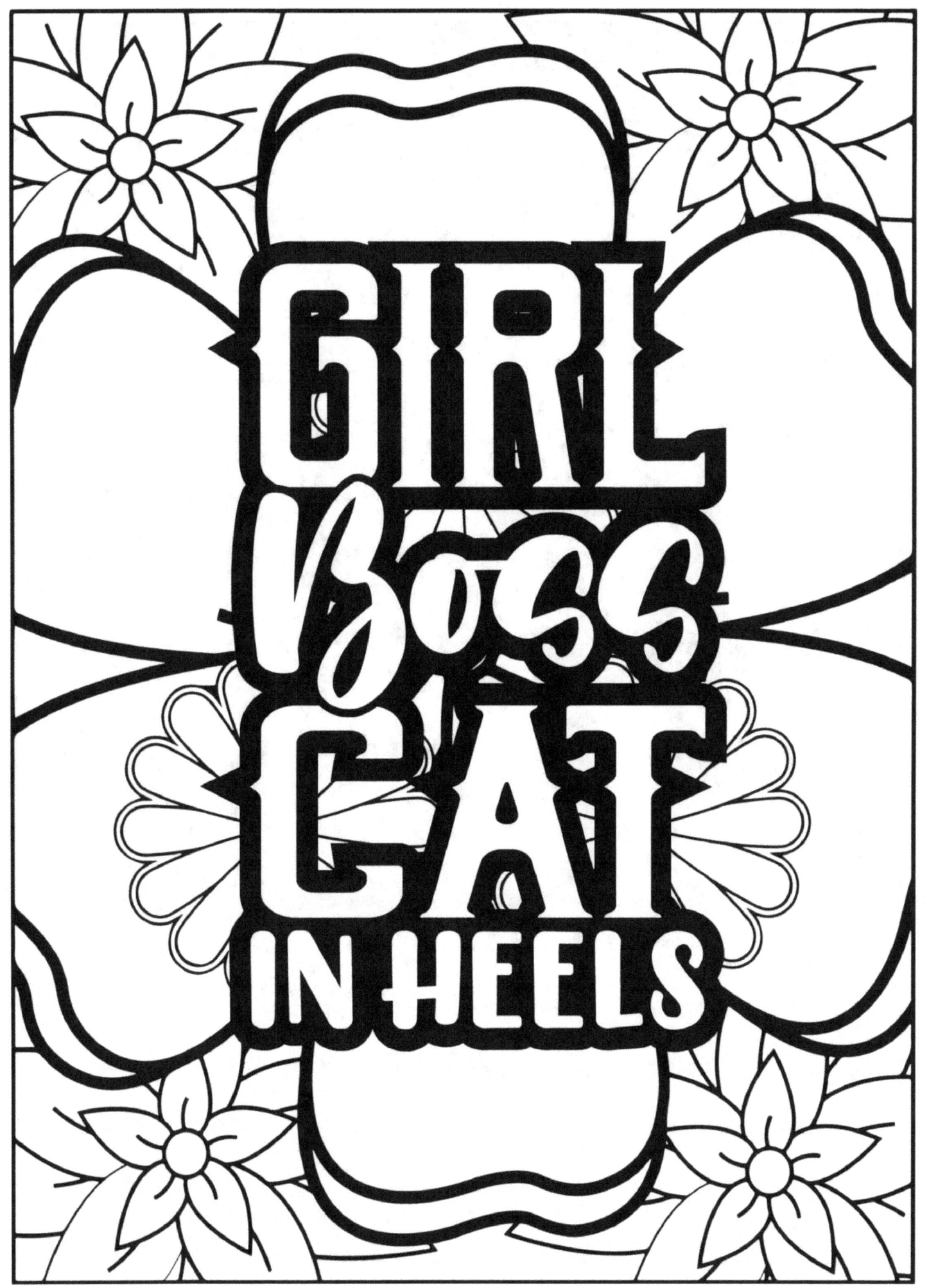

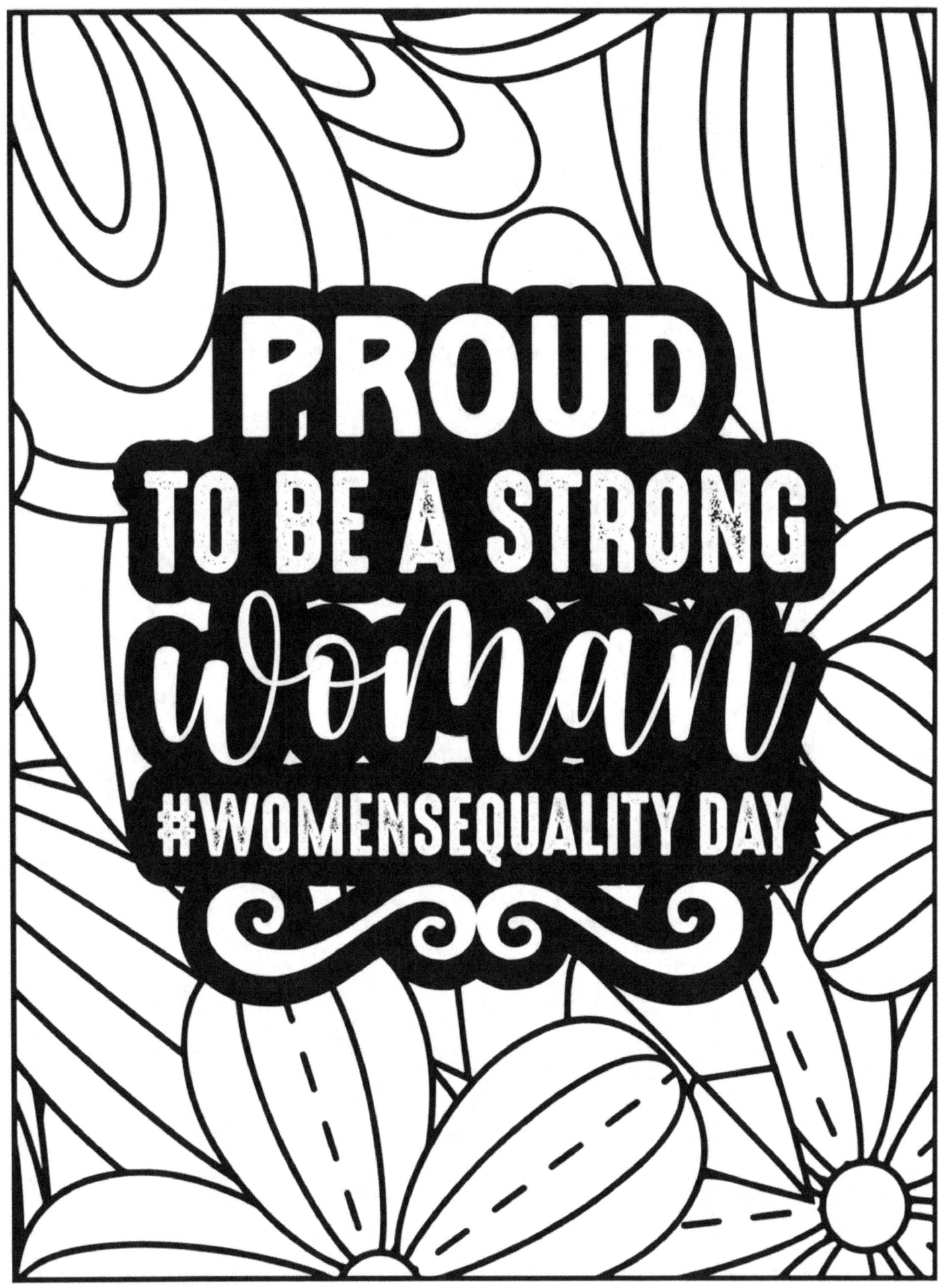

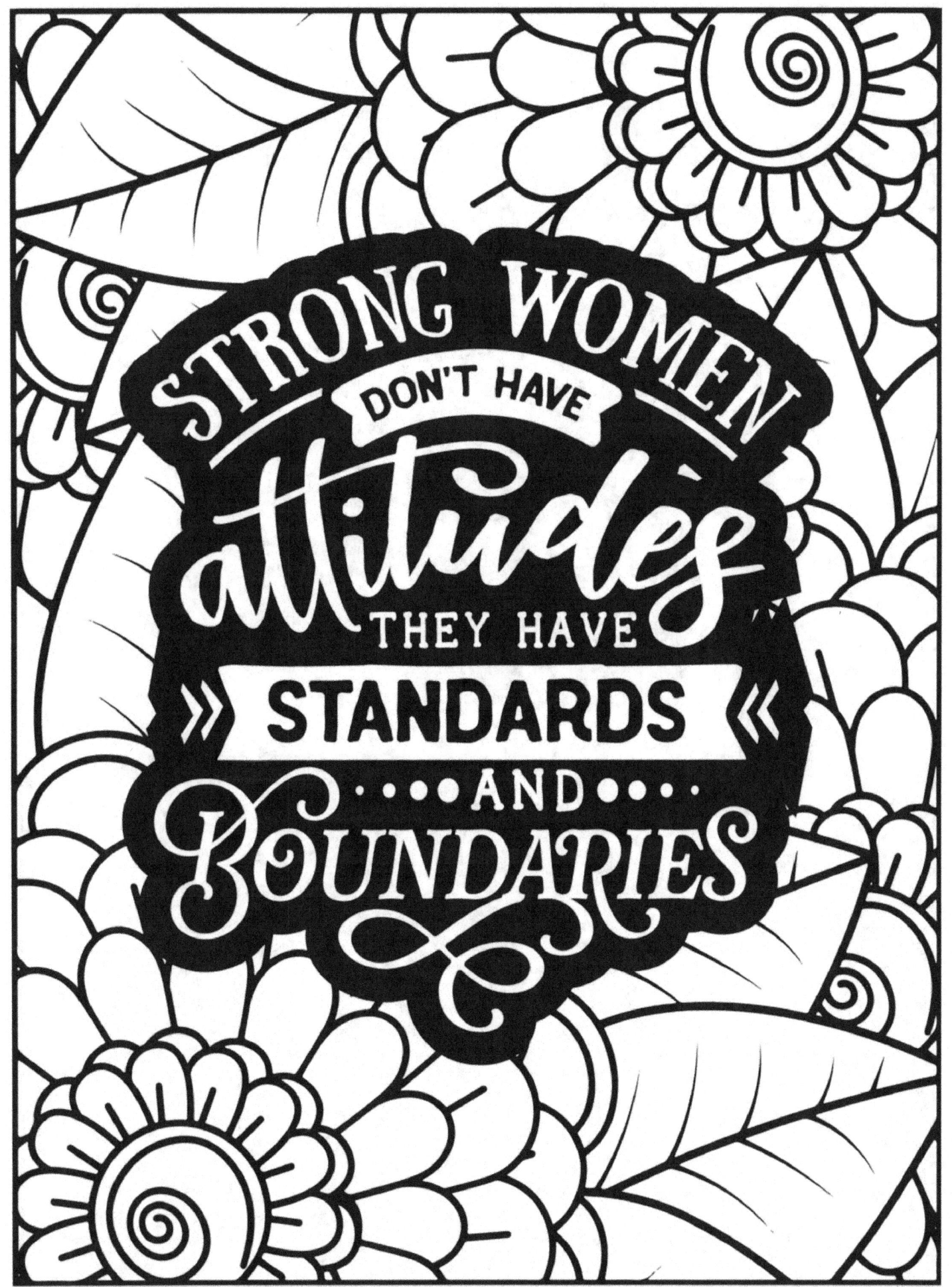

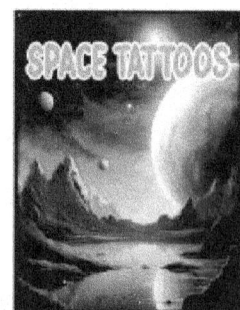